JASON'S STORY

Going to a Foster Home

by Deborah Anderson
and Martha Finne

Illustrated by Jeanette Swofford

Dillon Press, Inc.   Minneapolis, Minnesota 55415

To Judge George O. Petersen, presiding judge of Ramsey County, Minnesota Juvenile Court, and a member of the National Council of Juvenile and Family Court Judges

Illustrations courtesy of Hennepin County Medical Society Auxiliary, Inc.

Library of Congress Cataloging in Publication Data

Anderson, Deborah, 1946-
  Jason's story.

  Summary: Describes the experiences of a young boy in the foster care system.
  1. Foster home care—United States—Juvenile literature. 2. Child abuse—United States—Prevention—Juvenile literature. [1. Foster home care] I. Finne, Martha. II. Title.
  HV881.A65 1986   362.7'33'0973   85-25414
  ISBN 0-87518-324-7

Dillon Press, Inc., 242 Portland Avenue South
Minneapolis, Minnesota 55415

Printed in the United States of America
  2 3 4 5 6 7 8 9 10 95 94 93 92 91 90 89 88 87

Contents

Jason's Story

Jason is seven years old and lives with his mother. He is happy about that—he and his mother haven't always lived together. For part of his life, Jason lived with other families in foster homes. A foster home is a home where adults take care of other people's children.

When Jason was born in the hospital, he was a good baby, easy to care for. If he was hungry or tired, or if something didn't feel good, he cried. But just as soon as the hospital nurses fed him or put a dry diaper on him, he was fine. If they talked to him, held him, and kissed him, he was happy.

When Jason and his mother, Sheila, went home, Jason started to cry more often. He cried because he didn't get enough to eat and he was wet. His wet diapers gave him sores that hurt. He didn't get enough attention, either.

Jason's mother, Sheila, was young, only sixteen. Sheila didn't hold or kiss Jason very often. She didn't understand what babies need. Sheila didn't know it is important to give babies love and affection. Jason was boring, she thought, because all he did was sleep, cry, and eat. Sheila wanted to be with her friends. She didn't want to act like Jason's mother.

Jason and Sheila lived with Sheila's parents, Jason's grandparents. They had problems. Jason's grandma and grandpa got drunk a lot. They would yell and fight with each other and with Jason's mother. When there was a fight, Jason's mother would scream, "You can take care of him!" and leave the house. Lots of times, though, no one did take care of baby Jason after a fight. Jason's grandparents would be angry, so they would not help Jason.

Jason was in a family with terrible troubles.

When Jason was about two months old, Sheila took him to see his doctor, Dr. Brown, for a checkup. "Jason should weigh more than he does," said Dr. Brown to Sheila. "You need to see that he eats more. Jason should also have his diapers changed more often. Here's medicine for his bottom. I want you both to come back in two weeks."

The doctor told Sheila how to take care of Jason. But the problems at Jason's house went on. Nobody really wanted to take care of him. Jason's mother just wanted to be with her friends. Jason's grandparents were angry and didn't take care of Jason, either.

Every time Dr. Brown saw Jason, he saw that the problems weren't going away. When Jason was four months old, Dr. Brown called Child Protection Services. He said to a social worker there, "I think you should check on this baby, Jason Simmons. I've been seeing him every two weeks. He's not gaining weight as he should. I believe he isn't getting the care that he needs."

The next day, a social worker came to Jason's house. He asked questions, and soon found out about Jason's troubles. He saw that Jason wasn't getting enough of the things all babies need—food, dry clothes, and hugs and kisses. The social worker talked with Sheila about this. But Jason's mother said everything was just fine. Sheila was angry and said she didn't need help.

The social worker knew that Jason did need help, though. To get help, he went to a judge. In court, they made a decision about Jason. Since there was so much trouble at Jason's house, Jason should be put in a foster home. They said baby Jason was in danger where he was, so someone else would have to take care of him.

Jason was too young to know what foster homes were. He was too young to talk or understand if someone explained. When a child goes to a foster home, the people there take care of him or her as though he or she were their own child. Some foster parents have children of their own, and some don't. Usually, foster parents love children and want to take good care of them.

Jason went to live at the Bakers' house. Mr. and Mrs. Baker had two girls of their own, Ann and Selene. All of the Bakers just loved baby Jason! He got all the things he needed at the Bakers', especially love and attention. Ann and Selene treated Jason just like a little brother. Mr. and Mrs. Baker played with him, held him, fed him, and kept him clean and dry. Every few months a social worker would check on Jason, too.

Jason gained weight. He even became chubby! Jason was growing, too. Soon he was crawling and pulling himself up on furniture. Both Ann and Selene helped him walk by holding his hands.

By the time Jason was two years old, he was running and talking and saying no. He called Mrs. Baker "Mama" and Mr. Baker "Daddy"—just like Ann and Selene did. Jason didn't remember his real, birth mother. She never visited him. He thought Mrs. Baker was his mother.

One day, though, a social worker called Mrs. Baker. She told Mrs. Baker, "Jason's mother wants to see Jason."

As a foster mother, Mrs. Baker knew that someday Jason's real mother might want him again. When Mrs. Baker told Selene and Ann that Jason's real mother, Sheila, was coming to visit him on Saturday, both girls had questions.

Ann said, "I feel that Jason is really my brother, Mom. Can Sheila take him from us?"

"He calls you 'Mama', " said Selene. "How are you going to tell him you aren't his mom?"

"I'd better explain this to you girls again," said Mrs. Baker. "Remember when Jason first came to stay with us? We told you it wouldn't be forever. When he came, his mother wasn't caring for him very well. But she has solved some of her problems, and wants to see Jason again.

"We always knew that his mother might come back for him. We don't know what will happen right now. Even though we have gotten to love Jason as our own baby, he isn't ours. He is our foster child, and probably will go back to his mother," said Mrs. Baker.

All of the Bakers felt sad. All week everybody was extra close to Jason. On Friday, Mrs. Baker told Jason, "Tomorrow your real mommy is coming to see you." But Jason just didn't understand.

When Sheila, Jason's mother, came on Saturday to visit, she was happy to see Jason. Jason felt shy, so he stayed close to Mrs. Baker. Two-year-old Jason didn't know who this stranger was!

Over the next month, Jason's mother came more often. Then, she started to take Jason in the car with her. A few times she kept him overnight.

This was a hard time for Jason and the Bakers. Jason seemed to like Sheila, his mother, but he was just too little to understand what was happening. He liked to go out, but he always came back to the Bakers' house.

Finally, the day came for Jason to go and live with Sheila. It was time to say good-bye to the Baker family. Mrs. Baker cried, but tried not to show it to Jason. She said, "Bye, bye, sweetie. You grow up to be a good, big boy. We love you." Then she said, "Your mommy loves you a lot, too."

After all the Bakers hugged Jason, he and his mother went off together. Jason didn't understand that, this time, he would not go back to the Bakers' house.

Jason's mom was happy to have Jason back. "Now we're going to be a real family. I'll work hard at the store while you're at day care. The rest of the time we'll be together," she said.

All this change was hard for Jason. He was mixed up. Sometimes he asked for "Mommy." His mother would say, "I'm your mommy," but Jason would just cry. He wanted to be with Mrs. Baker. He missed all the Bakers and was sad that his "mommy," Mrs. Baker, didn't see him anymore.

Sheila found out that being a mother wasn't very easy. Two year olds can be stubborn—they don't always do what they are told to do. On some mornings, Jason wouldn't eat breakfast fast enough or would want to stay home. Then they were late to day care. Sheila's boss would yell at her when she came late to work because of Jason.

Still, one year and then another went by. Jason forgot about the Bakers. Jason's mother loved him, and he loved her back. Jason felt happy again.

When Jason was four, he had the chicken pox and was very sick. Jason's mother knew that someone had to stay with Jason. She called her social worker for help. "I can't help you," said the social worker. "You'll have to stay home and take care of him yourself."

In the end, Jason's mother had to stay home from work for four days. Her boss was angry with her. She almost lost her

job. And Jason's mother was angry at Jason. When she stayed home, she didn't get paid. That made it hard to pay for everything. She told Jason he was a bad boy for getting sick.

After that time, Jason and his mother were unhappy more and more often. Sometimes Jason would get into trouble at home. One day he put the towels in the toilet. It got plugged up, and water went all over the floor. Sheila was so angry she spanked Jason and locked him in the closet. He cried and screamed, but she wouldn't let him out. When he fell asleep, she put him to bed.

Another day, Jason wrote all over the walls with a crayon. That really made his mom angry. This time she hit him hard with a belt and left red marks on his back. Then, she put him in the closet. The next day, when Sheila picked Jason up from day care, the woman in charge asked her about the marks on Jason's back. "He fell down," Sheila said, even though she knew the marks were from the belt.

More and more, Sheila would get angry and hurt Jason with the belt. One afternoon when she went to pick Jason up at the day care center, a social worker was there. "I called Child Protection because I am worried about Jason," said the day care worker to Sheila. "He's hitting other children and having temper tantrums. That's not like him!" The day care worker had also seen many bruises on Jason's body.

The social worker from the Child Protection office met once with Jason's mother. But the social worker was very busy, and did not visit Jason and his mother at home. Nothing changed. Jason kept getting hit and locked up.

Because of her troubles, Jason's mother sometimes got drunk. Soon she was fired from her job. Now she had really big troubles—no job, and no money to pay for day care. Now there was no one to take care of Jason while she looked for a job. When Sheila had troubles, Jason had troubles, too. His mom was angry about her troubles. Even though Jason was just a little boy, she told Jason, "It's your fault that I don't have anything. Why are you so bad all the time?"

One day, Jason's mother left Jason alone all day when she went out to look for a job. When Sheila got back, she found another social worker at the apartment. A neighbor had heard Jason crying because he was all alone, and had called the Child Protection office.

This social worker asked Jason and his mother a lot of questions. When she learned that Sheila didn't have a job, the social worker was worried. They talked a long timc.

Finally, Sheila said she knew she had problems. She didn't have enough money for rent, she drank too much, and she couldn't take care of Jason all by herself. The problems were just too much for Sheila.

The social worker said, "Why don't we put Jason in a foster home while you get help with these problems?"

Sheila was tired from arguing. She agreed. "But just until I get a job," she said. "Then I want him with me."

The social worker talked to Jason alone then. She told him that his mother needed time to work out her problems. Because he was getting hurt so much, they needed to be apart for a while.

Jason's mother was sad and angry that night. She cried and drank. Jason really felt like a bad boy now, because his mother was so sad.

A few days later, the social worker

came to take Jason to the Johnsons'. "The Johnsons love to care for children," she said. "Right now they are caring for a little boy who's six and a girl who's eight. You'll meet the children when they come home from school."

"I don't want to go there," Jason said. He was scared and worried. "How long will I have to stay?"

"Well, Jason," said the worker. "I don't know how long, exactly, but you won't be there very long."

Jason was safer at the Johnsons. He was watched, and he wasn't hit with a belt or put in the closet. The Johnsons weren't as warm and loving as the Bakers. So Jason felt very alone. He loved his mother, and missed seeing her

every day. At first, he cried and threw
things. The Johnsons both told him to
stop, and Mrs. Johnson sent Jason to
his room until he could behave. Jason
finally knew he wouldn't be going home
right away, so he stopped his crying and
became very quiet all the time.

Jason's mother visited him a few times at the Johnsons' foster home. Jason was always glad to see her. But when the visits were over, they both felt sad. Sheila didn't want to leave Jason. She didn't have a job, though, and couldn't take him with her. She still had troubles.

Jason believed he was a very bad boy. He thought that his mother believed he was bad, too. After all, she wouldn't take him with her. He thought the Johnsons believed he was bad, because they didn't pay any attention to him.

Then, Sheila didn't come to visit Jason for weeks and weeks. No one talked to him about it—they thought he was too young to understand. Jason felt sad, lonely, scared—and bad.

One day when Jason returned from school, a new social worker was at the Johnsons' house. His name was Mr. Casey. It seemed to Jason that there were always new social workers. The older children at the Johnsons' were visited by social workers, too.

This social worker was different, though. He told Jason he was from the court, and that his job was to try to get kids and parents back together. He asked Jason to sit on the sofa and talk with him.

Mr. Casey said, "Jason, do you understand that your mom is having some big trouble?"

"Yes," said Jason quietly, looking at the floor.

"Do you know that you didn't make her trouble?" Mr. Casey asked him. Jason didn't answer.

Mr. Casey said, "Jason, when I was five years old, my mother had terrible trouble, just like your mother. I thought I was a bad boy, but I wasn't. I was a good boy, just like you are." He looked sad. "I lived in foster homes, too. Then I would be with my mother, and then go to another foster home. I went back and forth, just like you."

Jason just looked at Mr. Casey. Jason had really believed that he was a bad boy. He thought he made it hard for his mother. That's why she would drink. He was bad, and that was why his mother hit him and locked him in the closet.

Mr. Casey had something else to tell Jason. "Your mom has been getting help. She was in treatment. That was to help her stop drinking and work on some of her problems. Now she is going to a school that helps mothers learn to be a better mother." Jason just kept on listening. *Now* he knew why his mother didn't visit him!

Mr. Casey told Jason that his mother had a new job. "This job is a special job for mothers who have big troubles. At this job they pay special attention to mothers so they can work and take care of their children."

"When can I live with Mama again?" asked Jason.

"You'll start with visits," said Mr. Casey. "I'll come see you both to see how I can help get you back together. Your mother wants to be with you very much, Jason."

From then on, Jason and Sheila spent every Saturday together. It was strange at first. Even though they were mother and son, they had to get to know each other again.

Both of them had changed. Jason was more grown up. He was in school all day, not at day care. Sheila had worked hard on her problems. She didn't drink at all anymore, and she tried hard to control her anger—in fact, she was happy most of the time. Sheila had gotten a new apartment that had a bedroom for Jason.

After several months, Mr. Casey said Jason could live with his mother. Mr. Casey visited them every week. If there was a problem, he visited more often. Other people were helping them, too. Sheila got help at work, at home, and just for herself. Little by little, by working hard, Sheila solved most of her problems.

At last, she got a better job that paid her more money. She took good care of Jason and didn't leave him alone. When Jason did things he wasn't supposed to do, Sheila talked to him about what he did. She didn't hit or hurt him. He liked that.

Now, Jason was feeling more and more like a good boy. It had taken a long time, but his mother had changed. And the changes were just what Jason needed. He finally felt wanted and loved by his mother. He trusted that she wouldn't leave him anymore. Sheila had learned how to be a good mother to Jason.

Finally, at seven years old, Jason is with his family again. He and his mother went from having lots of bad troubles to just having little troubles, once in a while. Jason is glad about that.

Children and Foster Care

In the story, when Jason was a baby, he had to go to a foster home. He wasn't getting the things he needed to grow up healthy. Later, when he was four, his mother was physically abusing him, and he needed a safe place to live.

It is important to know that children are NOT put in foster care to punish them. Foster care is there when parents do not or cannot take care of their children.

Most of the families of children in

foster care have serious troubles, like Jason's did. Many don't get help for their troubles, or even know how to get help. Others may be very sick and not able to do day-to-day chores needed to help children grow up well.

Here are some things to know about foster care.

- Children in foster care come from many places. They are from rich and poor neighborhoods, from cities, small towns, and farm areas, and from families of every color and background.

- Many children are in foster homes for a long time, and many families don't get help with their problems like Sheila did. But foster care is not supposed to be permanent, or forever. Judges in juvenile court, who put children in foster homes, should make sure that families get help with their problems. Social workers usually are the ones who help families with problems.

- Children in foster care are supposed to be able to see their families. Sometimes that might not happen if a parent is very sick or in treatment.

- If and when the family's troubles are solved, the child will go back to the family. This is what everyone who helps is working for. If the troubles with the family can't be helped, then the child will not go back.

- Every child has the right to a chance to grow up in a loving family. When a judge decides that family troubles are too serious, and probably will not get better, then the child in foster care is given the chance to be adopted by a family that will love him or her.

Words to Know

adopt (uh·DAHPT)—to take someone else's child as a member of your family. Adopted children stay with their new family until they are grown

affection (uh·FEK·shun)—loving feelings shown by words and actions

attention (uh·TEN·shun)—here, attention is noticing a child and what that child is needing

Child Protection Services (CHYLD proh·TEK·shun SER·vih·sez)—a group of people whose jobs are to see that children are not being harmed by their families and that the children are getting

40

the things they need to grow up healthy and whole

court (KORT)—a meeting with a judge (and sometimes a jury) where the judge decides if someone has broken the law or if someone with serious problems should get help for those problems

diaper (DY·per)—cloth or paper that is put between a baby's legs and fastened around the waist so that it can soak up urine and feces when the baby goes to the bathroom

foster care (FAWS·ter KAYR)—care given to a child whose own family can't or doesn't give that child what he or she needs to grow up healthy and whole

foster home (FAWS·ter HOHM)—a place where a child lives with a family not related to him or her for a while. Here, the child is cared for by that family as if they were his or her family. The child does not usually stay with this family until he or she is grown

judge (JUHJ)—the person in charge of the court who sees that the rules of the court are obeyed, and who decides if someone has broken the law or if someone needs help for very serious problems

juvenile court (JOO·vuh·nyl KORT)—a special court for children (juveniles) under 18 years old who need help or who have broken the law

permanent (PER·muh·nent)—kept the same, with little change, for a very long time

physical abuse (FIHZ·ih·kuhl uh·BYOOS)—when an adult hurts a child and leaves marks, and it isn't an accident

social worker (SOH·shul WER·ker)—a person whose job is to help people with serious problems

treatment (TREET·ment)—special help for people. Treatment can be to help sick bodies get well, or it can be to help people who abuse others or themselves learn new ways to act

Note to Adults

In 1983, there were approximately 500,000 childen in foster care. That is about twice the number in foster care in 1976. As the government and the public become more and more aware of child abuse and neglect, the use of foster care escalates. Children do need to have a safe place to live, but the problem is that too many are being unnecessarily placed outside the family. Also, too many children in foster care drift from home to home, and no permanent plans are made for them.

Efforts are currently being made throughout the United States to prevent unnecessary placement of children. The National Council of Juvenile and Family Court Judges has been a leader of the movement to keep families together. They also have undertaken a Permanency Planning Project in response to a national law passed in 1980 that mandated followup on children in foster care. They are working on guidelines for permanent placement of children. Presently, the judges are attempting to help other judges, legislators, social workers, and lay child advocates work for changes in law, policy, and practice that will help ensure permanent homes for abused and neglected children.

In lieu of foster care placement of children, alternatives such as providing more and improved social services to families are now being tried. This is also being done for families that have been reunited.

Sometimes, returning children to their biological parents is not likely; many states are beginning to recognize that, and move toward permanent placement or adoption.

A hope in all of this is that fewer children in the future will need to be placed in foster care. Those who are placed will not be lost in the system, but monitored and planned for so they can grow up in a safe, permanent, nurturing environment and establish lifetime relationships.

How Adults Can Help

Children in out-of-home placement have a tremendous need for supportive, loving care from adults. There is always a shortage of foster parents for children of all ages. Those foster parents who are providing a warm, caring atmosphere for children need and deserve support from a wide variety of people. They do receive some financial compensation from the government, but it is impossible to put a price tag on a parent.

Volunteers are being utilized more and more in this field. Two volunteer programs currently in operation are Court-Appointed Special Advocates (CASA) and guardians *ad litem*. Both of these programs provide children with someone to act as their representative in legal proceedings revolving around child abuse, neglect, or out-of-home placement proceedings, and ensure a followup to the case. As of January, 1985, there were 110 CASA programs in 30 states.

More information on all of the above can be obtained from local county Human Services Departments.

About the Authors

Deborah Anderson, Executive Vice President of Responses, Inc., has helped establish programs to aid both children and adults whose lives have been touched by abuse and neglect. Deborah developed and directed a sexual assault services program for the Hennepin County (Minnesota) Attorney's Office, and created the conceptual basis for Illusion Theater's internationally acclaimed production, "Touch," which presents information on abuse to children. Deborah has worked with students, teachers, and school administrators regarding child abuse and neglect, and has been nationally recognized for her work in the area of children as victims or witnesses in court.

Martha Finne, Director of the Children's Division of Responses, Inc., joined that organization after directing a survey of Minneapolis school children entitled, "Child Abuse and Neglect: From the Perspectives of the Child," the basis for these books. She has worked as a child abuse consultant, speaking to parent groups and elementary school staffs regarding child abuse and its prevention. Her background includes a degree in social psychology, counseling at the Bridge for Runaway Youth, and volunteer experience working with both public schools and social service agencies.

About Responses, Inc.

Responses to End Abuse of Children, Inc. is a
public nonprofit corporation which tries to
coordinate programs in all segments of the
community aimed at reducing family violence
and child abuse and neglect. The organization
works with both the private and public sectors to
develop the most constructive responses to these
problems.

In 1983 and 1984 Responses, Inc. conducted a
survey of Minneapolis school children to assess
the children's knowledge on various aspects of
child abuse and neglect. The responses to the
survey provided the framework for these Child
Abuse books.